ADDITION

By CHARLES GHIGNA

Illustrations by MISA SABURI

Music by MARK OBLINGER

CANTATA
LEARNING

WWW.CANTATALEARNING.COM

CANTATA LEARNING

Published by Cantata Learning
1710 Roe Crest Drive
North Mankato, MN 56003
www.cantatalearning.com

Library of Congress Cataloging-in-Publication Data
Names: Ghigna, Charles. | Saburi, Misa, illustrator. | Oblinger, Mark.
Title: Addition / by Charles Ghigna ; illustrations by Misa Saburi ; music by
  Mark Oblinger.
Description: North Mankato, MN : Cantata Learning, [2018] | Series: Winter
  math | Audience: Age 3-8. | Audience: K to grade 3.
Identifiers: LCCN 2017007534 (print) | LCCN 2017016720 (ebook) | ISBN
  9781684100088 | ISBN 9781684100071 (hardcover : alk. paper)
Subjects: LCSH: Addition--Juvenile literature. | Arithmetic--Juvenile
  literature.
Classification: LCC QA115 (ebook) | LCC QA115 .G438 2018 (print) | DDC
  513.2/11--dc23
LC record available at https://lccn.loc.gov/2017007534

Book design, Tim Palin Creative
Editorial direction, Flat Sole Studio
Executive musical production and direction, Elizabeth Draper
Music arranged and produced by Mark Oblinger

Printed in the United States of America in North Mankato, Minnesota.
072017   0367CGF17

ACCESS THE MUSIC!
SCAN CODE WITH MOBILE APP
CANTATALEARNING.COM

TIPS TO SUPPORT LITERACY AT HOME

WHY READING AND SINGING WITH YOUR CHILD IS SO IMPORTANT

Daily reading with your child leads to increased academic achievement. Music and songs, specifically rhyming songs, are a fun and easy way to build early literacy and language development. Music skills correlate significantly with both phonological awareness and reading development. Singing helps build vocabulary and speech development. And reading and appreciating music together is a wonderful way to strengthen your relationship.

READ AND SING EVERY DAY!

TIPS FOR USING CANTATA LEARNING BOOKS AND SONGS DURING YOUR DAILY STORY TIME

1. As you sing and read, point out the different words on the page that rhyme. Suggest other words that rhyme.

2. Memorize simple rhymes such as Itsy Bitsy Spider and sing them together. This encourages comprehension skills and early literacy skills.

3. Use the questions in the back of each book to guide your singing and storytelling.

4. Read the included sheet music with your child while you listen to the song. How do the music notes correlate to the words of the song?

5. Sing along on the go and at home. Access music by scanning the QR code on each Cantata book. You can also stream or download the music for free to your computer, smartphone, or mobile device.

Devoting time to daily reading shows that you are available for your child. Together, you are building language, literacy, and listening skills.

Have fun reading and singing!

Come enjoy the winter season with the children in this story. They see some wonderful sights and do some fun things. Two **snow geese** fly overhead, and the children decorate 3 cookies. But how many more of these things do you need to make 10?

Turn the page to practice adding numbers. Remember to sing along.

Adding numbers with our friends—
let's add numbers to make 10!

Let's add 1 + 9.

Now we have 10 pinecones
all in a line.

Let's add 2 + 8.

Now we have 10 snow geese swimming in a lake.

Let's add 3 + 7.

Now we have 10 cookies
hot from the oven.

13

Let's add 4 + 6.

Now we have 10 candles in **candlesticks!**

Let's add 5 + 5.

Now we have 10 snowmen
with charcoal eyes!

There are many ways to make ten.

Let's repeat them all again!

$$1 + 9 = 10$$

$$2 + 8 = 10$$

$$3 + 7 = 10$$

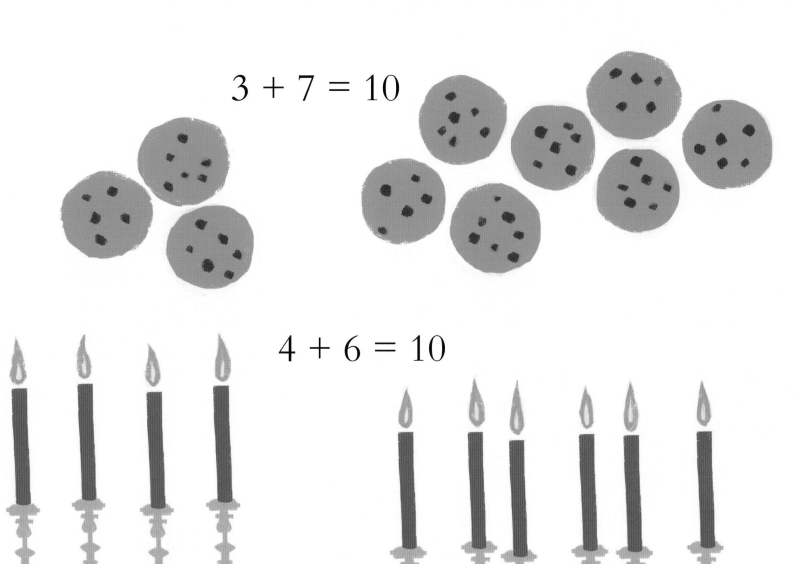

$$4 + 6 = 10$$

$$5 + 5 = 10$$

Adding numbers with our friends—
We added numbers to make 10!
We added numbers to make 10!
We added numbers to make 10!

21

SONG LYRICS
Addition

Adding numbers with our friends—
Let's add numbers to make 10!

Let's add 1 + 9.
Now we have 10 pine cones
all in a line.

Let's add 2 + 8.
Now we have 10 snow geese
swimming in a lake.

Let's add 3 + 7.
Now we have 10 cookies
hot from the oven.

Let's add 4 + 6.
Now we have 10 candles
in candlesticks!

Let's add 5 + 5.
Now we have 10 snowmen
with charcoal eyes!

There are many ways to make ten.
Let's repeat them all again!
1 + 9 = 10
2 + 8 = 10
3 + 7 = 10
4 + 6 = 10
5 + 5 = 10

Adding numbers with our friends—
We added numbers to make 10!
We added numbers to make 10!
We added numbers to make 10!

Addition

Jazz
Mark Oblinger

Intro

Add - ing num - bers with our friends — Let's add num - bers to make ten!

Interlude

Verse

1. Let's add one plus nine. Now we have ten pine - cones all in a line.

Interlude

Verse 2
Let's add 2 + 8.
Now we have 10 snow geese
swimming in a lake.

Interlude

Verse 3
Let's add 3 + 7.
Now we have 10 cookies
hot from the oven.

Interlude

Verse 4
Let's add 4 + 6.
Now we have 10 candles
in candlesticks!

Interlude

Verse 5
Let's add 5 + 5.
Now we have 10 snowmen
with charcoal eyes!

Interlude

Bridge

There are man - y ways to make ten. Let's re - peat them all a - gain! One plus nine e - quals ten! Two plus eight e - quals ten! Three plus sev - en e - quals ten! Four plus six e - quals ten! Five plus five e - quals ten!

Interlude

Outro

Add - ing num - bers with our friends — We add - ed num - bers to make ten! We add - ed num - bers to make ten! We add - ed num - bers to make ten!

GLOSSARY

candlesticks—holders for candles

snow geese—a species of geese with white feathers

GUIDED READING ACTIVITIES

1. What is winter like where you live? What activities do you do in the winter? Which animals do you see in the winter? Do you celebrate any special holidays in winter?

2. What is your favorite winter item in this song? Draw a picture with ten of those items.

3. How high can you count? Can you count past ten? Start counting to find out!

TO LEARN MORE

Anderson, Steven. *Ten Pigs in a Bed*. North Mankato, MN: Cantata Learning, 2016.

Clay, Kathryn. *All About Snowmen*. North Mankato, MN: Capstone, 2016.

Rissman, Rebecca, and Michael Nunn. *Counting 1 to 10*. Chicago: Heinemann-Raintree, 2012.

Weakland, Mark. *Hockey Counting*. North Mankato, MN: Capstone Press, 2014.